For Ann and Paul Krouse who have encouraged
and supported this writer every step of the way,
starting with my very first word: more. —A. K. R.

To Scotti Lichtenheld, the best mom a guy could hope for. —T. L.

Text copyright © 2015 by Amy Krouse Rosenthal.
Illustrations copyright © 2015 by Tom Lichtenheld.
All rights reserved. No part of this book may be reproduced in
any form without written permission from the publisher.

Library of Congress Cataloging-in-Publication Data:
Rosenthal, Amy Krouse, author.
I wish you more / by Amy Krouse Rosenthal ;
illustrated by Tom Lichtenheld.
pages cm
Summary: In simple text and pictures, the author and
illustrator create a compendium of small daily moments.
ISBN 978-1-4521-2699-9 (alk. paper)
1. Wishes—Juvenile fiction. [1. Wishes—Fiction.
2. English language—Comparison—Fiction.]
I. Lichtenheld, Tom, illustrator. II. Title.
PZ7.R719445Iak 2015
[E]—dc23

2013038165

Manufactured in China.

Design by Sara Gillingham Studio.
Typeset in Cabrito and Grenale.
The illustrations in this book were rendered
in ink, watercolor, pan pastels, and colored pencils,
with digital art assistance from Kristen Cella.

30 29 28 27 26 25 24 23 22

Chronicle Books LLC
680 Second Street
San Francisco, California 94107

Chronicle Books—we see things differently.
Become part of our community at www.chroniclekids.com.

I Wish You More

AMY KROUSE ROSENTHAL & TOM LICHTENHELD

chronicle books · san francisco

I wish you more ups
than downs.

I wish you more give than take.

I wish you more tippy-toes

than deep.

I wish you more we than me.

I wish you more hugs than ughs.

I wish you more WOO-HOO! than WHOA!

I wish you more will than hill.

I wish you more can than knot.

I wish you more snowflakes

than tongue.

I wish you more pause

than fast-forward.

I wish you more umbrella than rain.

I wish you more bubbles than bath.

I wish you more treasures

than pockets.

I wish you more stories than stars.

I wish all of this for you,

because you are everything
I could wish for . . .

and more.